The Mind

The Mind

The Pulpit of GOD

Pastor M.E. Lyons

AuthorHouse™
1663 Liberty Drive
Bloomington, IN 47403
www.authorhouse.com
Phone: 1-800-839-8640

Published by AuthorHouse   04/04/2012

ISBN: 978-1-4685-7662-7 (sc)
ISBN: 978-1-4685-7661-0 (hc)
ISBN: 978-1-4685-7660-3 (e)

Library of Congress Control Number: 2012905959

CONTENTS

Dedication vii

Preface ix

Acknowledgements.............................xiii

Foreword..xvii

Introduction... xxi

1. Temptation Is Still Here 1

2. It's All In The Mind 11

3. What's On Your Mind? 25

4. I Know Who I Am.................................... 37

5. Are You Out Of Your Mind? 49

6. Do The Right Thing................................. 57

7. There's No Place Like Home..................... 67

8. Other Book(s) Written/Published 77

DEDICATION

To Pastors and Preachers, Evangelists, Teachers, Laity who allow their minds to be filled with the wealth of knowledge in order that their minds can be used to benefit souls for the Kingdom's sake.

To Alice Starr my late Great Grandmother who instilled so much in me and my ministry by her commitment to Christ.

PREFACE

This book has been inspired of God to speak about the intimacies of the relationship between the mind and the proverbial pulpit of our lives. It is in the very cogitations of our minds that God intends to use our minds as a platform to push the very principles and directives of this Christian life we are all to live after coming into the knowledge and understanding of Christ. Through our minds are birthed specific instances to allow the Word of God to matriculate through the processes of our thoughts into the spiritual bloodstream of our deeds.

In this book, we will discuss and share messages, applications, and shared stories that will show evidence how through scripture, God is desirous to use our minds as an avenue to reach those who are in need of pulling from their individual pits in a psychological and even more emotional way.

We will venture to discuss and explain as the Holy Spirit gives utterance, how the mind works as a place where many will not allow God to mount the sacred desk of our minds, simply by the way we think, act, and carry out the cognitive reasoning processes on a daily basis.

This book is sure to highlight the necessity of following what Paul shares with Timothy when he speaks of, "*letting this mind be in you that was also in Christ Jesus*". This is the key in allowing our minds to serve as God's pulpit. The truth of the matter is that if God cannot mount the pulpit of our mind, He will find a mind that is waiting, willing, and welcoming for His mandate to be carried out. He seeks those who have a mind with a vacant pulpit. (*Revelation 3:20*)

ACKNOWLEDGEMENTS

To my wife, LaTish, words cannot express how much you mean to our ministry. You are a true administrative genius, God truly blessed me with you.

To my children, Deja, Myron, and Jeremiah, I love you and pray and expect great spiritually driven things from you.

To a very special family friend, Ms. Jessica "Ca" Nesmith, you have been a tremendous help with this project and have done an immaculate job. We pray

God's choicest blessings upon you for investing your gift into this book.

To my mentor, Dr. Lelious A. Johnson, thank you for being a man of wise counsel in our life. I hear ringing in my ear, "Thou art my everlasting portion". God bless you for your guidance and advice!

I would like to say thank you to the Goodwill Missionary Baptist Church Family for allowing me to serve as your leader. This privilege has helped me to grow in the areas needed in order that I might embrace the gifts God has deposited into my life!

To my friend and brother, Reverend Charleston L. Mayes, you have displayed what it is to be a man of faith. I have grown tremendously into whom God would have me to be, through hearing your testimony and gift, thanks my brother!

FOREWORD

I have read through the manuscript, THE MIND: THE PULPIT OF GOD, and found it quite refreshing that one of my sons dares to "write it out", what God has given him. This he has done for all to read and consider.

Pastor M.E. Lyons, young of age but mature in Spirit, started preaching as a young lad and has grown to be a mature pastor, burdened to proclaim the Word of God through his preachments, and teachments. He takes it to the next level by writing it down for us and others to *read, even to our personal benefit. Thank you pastor for your Holy Boldness, and your shepherd's heart!*

To those who will read this book, you will see that this preacher labors to help us understand that God breathes upon our minds to mold our lives into Christ-likeness. This shaping of the mind is a process requiring "dusk and deity." Our disciplines in the Word of God, coupled with our cooperation with that Word is indeed required. The more the Holy Spirit illuminates our understanding of the Word of God, the more He enables us to "do the Word" in everyday life.

Thank you Pastor Lyons for the challenges presented in this book. I applaud your efforts to stay on point, as you wrestle with this great theme. As I say to all young preachers, "He who reads will always have something to say." Keep reading and writing and God will continue to pour into you that which He wills for you to pour into the lives of others.

I remember the Late Dr. Manual Scott saying, "We need more of our preachers to write, write their experiences in the Word, and their understandings of the Word, so others can have a better walk with Jesus. This is a wonderful beginning for you. We shall watch and pray to see what else the Lord will give you for us.

I do encourage the reading public to read this book, prayerfully, that God may speak through it to you, and through it and you to others.

Remember, ". . . As a man thinketh in his heart, so is he." Pastor Lyons is challenging us to keep our minds stayed on Jesus. May our Christian disciplines, breathed on by the Holy Spirit, help us to do just that!

Stephen C. Nash, PhD

Pastor, Mt. Tabor Baptist Church

Dallas, Texas

March 27, 2012

INTRODUCTION

~ How can my mind be the pulpit of God? ~

The Mind is a very peculiar and strange work of art. Whoever coined the cliché that a mind is a terrible thing to waste; was on target. It actually has literally become the control center of not only our physical vehicle of actions and lifestyle, but it interestingly so; has become the place where God can mount and speak to others; but there can be no presentation from our minds if there is not a willing acceptance in our "LABE" which in translation means our heart. In Revelation 3: 20 it speaks to a knock, a door, and a Savior. Our Savior whom happens to be part of the God-head stands KNOCKING . . . awaiting entry . . . He will not obtrude, nor will He force entry, neither will He push His way into any situation, life, or thought. In this book, we will discover upon examination of several scriptures . . . the choice is ours whether or not we allow Him in . . . in a psychological and even logical manner. God desires to use this grey matter that rests between our ears to reach the length and breadth of this world. But how can he stand where we first will not welcome Him in, and secondly have no room. As you will come to find out; God will not stand in a crowded space . . .

1

Temptation Is Still Here

"I find then a law, that, when I would do

good, evil is present with me."

Romans 7:21

I have thought about this concept for some time now and the verdict is, we all have, are, and will be guilty of facing temptation at some juncture in our lives. When we begin to decipher and deal with this dialogue that Paul teaches in the aforementioned scripture, Paul takes the initiative and shares with us that even though thousands of years have passed, the problem in the Bible days and the problems today, are similar as it relates to our mind.

There is a struggle that we all share, whether it be ommissive or commissive, hidden or exposed. every person that is to read this literary work will be the victim of one of the most overlooked and underestimated enemies of all times, TEMPTATION. Temptation is a very sneaky, sensitive, and for many, an acceptable sin itself. It really becomes a more dressed up word for sin. Think about it; you are walking around and decide to sit down and eat and delve into the delicious food and before you know it you are full; but because temptation is more acceptable than sin in our minds; we continue and fall victim to a sin without ever acknowledging it. Once we have acknowledged this behavior we label it and overlook the shortcomings by saying, *that is a temptation of mine.*

Perhaps that vehicle did not carry your temptation. Well, what about when you are in church or a social gathering and see an exceptionally beautiful woman or outwardly handsome gentleman and know that you are married and take one look and then instead of looking away and gathering your mind; you continue to set your eyes upon them in a lustful way. What happens is that because we feel as though it has been localized in the human mind; we lessen the incident by saying he or she is my flavor or *that is a temptation of mine*. Inevitably, we have already succumbed to the trick of the enemy and are on our way to swallowing the bait which now has a better hold of us allowing us to be reeled in.

Paul teaches us that in this verse that temptation is just as much a sin than actually committing the sin. One of the worst things a Christian can do is entertain the thought of sin. Entertaining the thought of sin creates the experience of sin, and when the experience has been created, all that is now needed, is an opportunity to or fall for the manifestation of the sin. Sin, through the vehicle of temptation is very crafty, sneaky, and alluring, and not to mention temptation avails itself at all times, in one form or another. This is why satan uses our mind to weigh down the very thought of self sufficiency through Christ.

When the evils of this life attempts to gain the reigns of our mind, it opens a realm of sin that is difficult to avoid. This is one of the many reasons Paul says . . ."*I find then a law . . .*" He is saying that he has found a law for the simple fact that this is not an easy thing to shake, it is no joke, it is not a simplistic outlet, nor is it quick to process, this is a law. There must be great strides and endeavors to ready one's mind when they turn aside and confront and look into the evil eyes of temptation and say, no thank you. There must be a conviction harbored in one's heart to confidently know that when temptation has lifted its seductive yet ill-gotten appearances above the surface of thoughts in our mind that what is, cannot be compared to what shall be.

Many times in my own life, there have been times that things appeared much more appealing than they really were, only to find out that the picture was only a mirage. Temptation works similar to that. No matter how engaging or inviting it may seem, the end result is always worse. That is why Paul speaks of an attitude, we should take it into consideration when he says, *"when I would do good . . ."* Otherwise, my mind was made up, my thoughts were in order, and the direction was mapped out, but temptation has a way of messing up your mind, tainting your thoughts, and changing your direction.

Temp, is the term which indicates the climate in a room. So when we speak of this subject matter, it determines the climate in our lives. Will we fall victim to it, or will we stay the course? Will we be those that the temp determines our direction, or will we be those who will remain who we are destined to be, even in the midst of heated situations? We cannot expect Sunday morning favor while our mind is clouded with Saturday night fever. One of the most dangerous mechanisms of mistakes is that of the maneuvering of our misguided minds. If you absolutely want to know what powerfully pulls you from sanity to schizophrenia, it is the battle going on in the mind. There is but a thin line of division between having a clear mind and having a clouded mind. The deciding factor in whether or not we do the right thing or we do the wrong thing is based upon our minds. If you don't believe me, think about some instance in your life, where you had to make some very important decisions. Now in making the decisions, you had to talk it over with yourself before coming to a conclusion. Why is it that when we are making decisions we contemplate in our minds what to do, and then talk it over with ourselves. It is because, that which we know we should do is wrestling with that which know we should not to do. The fact of the matter is, our mind has us struggling on a daily basis with our own selves.

Paul says that there are two things tugging at my mind. The reality of this struggle is that we are all faced with temptations. We need to recognize that it is evident in all of our lives, and then we can handle it accordingly. We must allow Jesus to stand in the place that the battle is being fought. We should fill our minds with Christ, so that we may positively affect those who surround us.

Consider this metaphorically speaking; if our minds can serve as pulpits, our mouths become the speakers God desires to use. I have come to find out in my studies that our minds are really not our spiritual control panels, our ears are. Whoever controls that panel has direct access to our minds. What happens here is that whatever comes through our control panels, our ears; and filtered in our minds, will be magnified through our mouth. No one can control your mind unless you give them your control panel, unless you lend them your ear. By doing this it actually transforms your mind from being simply a *pit* to being a *pulpit*.

2

It's All In The Mind

Let this mind be in you,

which was also in Christ Jesus:

Who, being in the form of God, thought it

not robbery to be equal with God: But made

himself of no reputation, and took upon him

the form of a servant, and was made in the

likeness of men: And being found in fashion

as a man, he humbled himself, and became

obedient unto death, even the death of the

cross. Wherefore God also hath highly exalted him, and given him a name which is above every name: That at the name of Jesus every knee should bow, of things in heaven, and things in earth, and things under the earth;

Philippians 2:5-10

The mind is a strange subject, primarily because in this text it speaks of putting away one mind in order to replace it with *this* mind. One major issue that sweeps our communities, environments, and even our churches, is that of having the wrong mind-set or mentality. We have the wrong mentality because have not allowed the correct mind to be in us! When we are bent on thinking, behaving, and even speaking our mind, we actually evict God from a place He desires to be. We already know that He will not force His way into any situation, He would rather be welcomed. Many times in my own life I have found that my thoughts only make things more complex, my ways can only muddy the situation. It is only when I had completely become submissive in letting His mind be priority that things begin to fall in place. I remember one instance in my first pastorate I thought I knew how to go about making changes and even attempting to do what I thought needed to be done. If I would have let His mind become dominant, perhaps things would have turned out differently. Our minds complicate marriages, families, and sometimes even memberships because sometimes our minds are geared toward personal gain rather than spiritual gain.

In this 2nd chapter of Philippians, we find that the writer Paul is incarcerated. He is saying that we do not have to argue about anything. Be concerned about others *(verse 4)*. When we look at the book of Philippians we see an ambiguity of the all-sufficiency of Christ. This means that He is always sufficient or enough.

Is it not peculiar to look at the text and to see that Paul is writing to a people who are free, and encouraging them, yet while he is bound in prison. Paul takes the opportunity to author this book of encouragement, which is defined as a book of rejoicing. Even though the writer is incarcerated waiting to attend trial with that egotistic and ever hateful Nero, he yet writes letters indicating the joy that they should possess because of their relationship with God. I find this very uplifting because we have a proclivity to partake a spirit of depression when things are not going our way. When you really think about it, those of us who walk with God can usually accept the consequences when we have done something wrong. But when we have done nothing and hard times come, we have a tendency to get angry with God.

Paul's attitude throughout this whole ordeal is, *to live is Christ and to die is gain.* He is saying that, it does not matter what is done to him, he is prepared for the inevitable. You see Paul is not the kind of guy you want to hang out with if you do not like commitment. Can you imagine being in the prison cell with him, you are trying to get him to keep silent, and all Paul wants to talk about is Jesus? Nero is killing people for talking about Jesus. Would you admit to being with Paul? Some of us would tell Paul to pray quietly. Have you ever been with anybody who is just on fire for the Lord, a walking inferno? It did not matter where they were, they could be in the grocery store, and scream, *"thank you Jesus"*, or they would start dancing on their job. You may know someone that would begin to speak in tongues while you are on the phone with them. This is how Paul was. It did not matter to Paul, he was in it for one reason and that was to praise the name of the Lord. You have to understand that it takes a certain spiritual depth to praise God in spite of circumstances. God does not want a circumstantial praise, he wants a positional praise. Paul's ties were so deeply rooted in God, he was so anchored in God that no matter what was going on, on the surface, he found praise. The devil needs to realize that if God brought me out once, then the struggles I face now do not scare me. If I came out of a ditch once, what can you say to me about how I should praise God or when to praise God? Paul knew that if God desired to deliver him out of prison, He would, and when you know God like that, you can lift Him up no matter what. This is why he said, *"be anxious for nothing but in all things . . ."*

You are operating in the Spirit, when everything natural and material is working against you and you can still find praise. When you have no money, you can still find praise. When your friends have turned their backs on you, you can still find praise. When everything in your life is going wrong, you can find praise. When your family is on the verge of breaking up, you can still find praise. Praises release the blessings of God.

Paul reminds us that we should be able to help others. You may not be the greatest speaker, but you should be able to encourage someone. Your life may be in shackles, but you should have something to give to someone that is in greater need than you. At times, it seems like everything is going wrong all at the same time. Your boss is on your trail, your kids start acting out, the dog is barking at the wrong times, all of the sudden the car breaks down. Things are going wrong, and it causes you to lose your focus. Paul is saying you have to be on one accord, *let this mind be in you . . .*" Whenever there is a breakdown in situations that should be working together, they become splinters with everything else. Paul says, there is a need for togetherness in the church at Philippi. When we come into the house of God we should have one thing in common and that is to praise His name. I do not have to speak like you, I do not have to drive the same kind of car that you may drive, I do not have to be like you, I just have to come in with praise on my lips. As long as we are together, the devil cannot divide the house of worship. You can speak with your eloquent levels of linguistics. I can say three letter words, and He hears me just the same. If we all are coming for the right reason, satan does not have a chance.

Now let us look at this word *fellowship*. If we are going to come together and fellowship, there has to be a common denominator. That common ground is Jesus. Many of us come to church for the wrong reason. We come looking for a man, you are and will end up having some competition, and then you are going to start coming mad due to eye service. You know that's when we have eye trouble. Same thing for men, if you come looking for a woman; *(looking at somebody else that doesn't belong to us);* you start looking at her finger to see if she's married, how many kids she has? So now you spent all of service doing a background check on her & forgot all about Jesus. Understand this concept; when the spirit takes control; I won't shoot you the finger, I won't curse you out, I won't look at you crazy, I won't give you a piece of my mind. Because if I keep giving you a piece of my mind, soon I won't have any for myself. Some Churches even have some folk fighting over the smallest things in church, you're sitting in my seat; you know I sit here every Sunday. Our minds are simply clustered with menial and meaningless advances.

You see beloved our minds as it relates to these scriptures we now examine; they hinge on the three letter word of let! This small word may be small in length but large in meaning. Many times the war is waged when we wrestle with whether or not we will *LET* the right mind prevail.

I remember one specific time in ministry as I was Pastoring how there was gentleman who was hell bent on allowing his mind to being his superior front. What this does is cause friction; it creates a struggle between what is priority in the individuals life and achievements that it absolutely voices that I expect more from my way of doing things than God's way of doing things. Well, needless to say, God will always prevail in any situation when we *LET* His mind become superior. Watch how Paul expresses this thought: "Let this mind be **IN** you". How obvious it is what Paul desires for us to do. He simply says I know there are others around you that want you to think like them; they want you to take on their way of doing things and ultimately it births an all out war with God. We cannot win a war with God. Secondly, in evaluating the word **IN** Paul really suggests the same thing we offer in this book and that is don't allow Christ to be knocking on the door when your Pulpit should be vacant for Him to mount it, because what will happen is if God is not **IN** it's obvious; He's out. Whenever He is out anything can happen in the Mind. Remember the writer addressing this thought: "An idle mind is the devil's workshop". Otherwise a mind that has not God has become idle, because you can nowhere but become a person who has allowed satan to mount our minds! Beloved when we do not have the Mind of Christ dwell in us it sets an atmosphere of my

way or the highway; and this is dangerous, because

it suggests that God ways does not matter at all.

3

What's On Your Mind?

"Thou wilt keep him in perfect peace, whose

mind is stayed on thee: because he

trusteth in thee."

Isaiah 26:3

Could it be that problems have rushed in and inundated your mind? Could it be that a family member that have you repeatedly tried to help seems to continuously cause greater frustrations to stand guard at the door of your mind? Perhaps it is finances that have you contemplating whether or not a second or third job is needed? All of these aforementioned questions are the polar opposite of what Isaiah wishes for us to leave this setting with. The prophet suggests that we can alleviate our minds of the ills and qualms that we struggle with from day to day.

The greatest tragedy of our time is that of satan playing with our mind. It started in the Garden of Eden. What plagues our land are the problems that originate in our minds. Our minds are sensitive to what is taking place around us. It is the processor of human emotions. It tells us how to think, feel, react and often control our senses. It can be deceived, but it also can be deceptive, that is why one secular

songwriter says, your mind is playing tricks on you.

I have a simple question for you, *"what's on your*

mind?" Are your faculties focused on burdensome

bills? Has your psyche *(mind)* run 7back to the fun

you experienced last night? Does your sagacity or

better yet mind wonder how you are going to make

a relationship work that is beyond humanistic

repair? Your thoughts may be tied to a spousal or

parental argument, and upsetting you so much

you have been discouraged. I really do not know, it

could be a multiplicity of things, but the question

I really would love to be entertained is, "what's on

your mind?"

I am a witness that every time I enter into the church, my mind is not always on church. Every now and then, I need a paradisiacal psychoanalysis. It has become an epidemic that we come to church as a break from all the madness we left at home, or on the job, or elsewhere. If your mind is somewhere other than on God, it is in the wrong place. Isaiah, the bold and courageous prophet said, *"thou wilt keep him in perfect peace, whose mind stayed on thee; because he trusteth in thee"*. We can never avoid strife and struggles, but we can certainly have peace of mind while we experience strife and struggles. We have to have a constant commercial break, when our mind begins to play tricks on us. I have to keep Him on my mind. When my bills are greater than my income, it is time for a commercial break, *"but my God shall supply . . .*" When the doctor gives me some troubling news, it is time for a commercial break, *"I am the God that healeth thee"*. When I feel like waving the white flag of surrender, it is time for a commercial break, *"I am more than a conqueror . . ."* When my name is being scandalized, it is time for a commercial break, *"I will make your enemies your footstools"*. When I begin to think unholy thoughts, it is time for a commercial break, *"An idle mind is the devil's workshop"*. The word "keep" means, to guard or protect. If we keep our mind stayed on Him, He will protect us, guard us and keep us in His perfect peace.

Initially, there seeps out of the treasures of this scripture: close communication. When you look intensely at this scripture, you will see that the more you talk to Him the easier it is to rid yourself of the throws of this world. Consider this; there is a difference in speaking to someone with small talk and someone whereas the conversation has a lingering love. When someone creates small talk, that conversation is only taking place because they have some spare time and there is no one else around to speak to. On the other hand, when you speak with someone with close communication, it denotes that what you have to say has significance.

Isaiah presents to us the remedy and anecdote of how to live a stress free life! He simply says, *"Thou wilt keep you in perfect peace . . . whose mind"*. When he speaks of this mind, it means that if you will continuously talk to Him not as if you are just trying to pass time but, if you enjoy and are benefitted when you speak to Him, your mind will rest in peace. How many times has talking to God simply relaxed your mind, calmed your spirit, and even turned the valve off to your tears?

The Prophet Isaiah is trying to convey to us that in this particular scripture what we think is what we say, and most times what we say is what we think. In essence, if we can continuously think about Him, we cannot help but talk to Him.

Secondly, you need a DIVINE DISPOSITION. Do you see it there? *"Thou wilt keep him in perfect peace whose mind is stayed on thee . . ."* The mind in one context is our neurological expression, but here mind represents our lifestyle. Ephesians 2:10, *"For we are his workmanship created in Christ Jesus unto good works . . ."* We were created to live Holy. The word workmanship derives from the Greek word *poience,* which derives from the word poem, which is the ancient word of poet; which means we are his masterpieces. When God spoke everything into existence, light started skipping across backdrop of the night, water began to run into hands of the earth, birds gained confidence and spread their wings and flew. But when it came to man, he stopped and said boys, let us. Whoever lives according to the masterpiece He has made, will have peace. If you are to have this peace you must have a divine disposition.

The keyword in the text is *stayed*. There has to be constancy in keeping your mind on Him. If we are fickled with our minds and allow our minds to go here and there, it will be as if we are standing on a shaky platform. It is inevitable that the platform will collapse underneath us.

The writer could have said thou wilt keep him in perfect peace who thinks, instead of "stayed". This would simply indicate that He comes to mind every now and again. He could have said remember, instead of "stayed". This would indicate that it only happens when something triggers your mind to lead you to focus on Him. But Isaiah says *stayed*. The word stayed, yields that we should lean on Him all of the time. This brings to mind that old yet rich song many of us heard practically every Sunday morning during morning worship, *I woke up this morning with my mind stayed on Him, I'm walking and talking with my mind, stayed on him. Singing and praying with my mind, stayed on him. It ain't no harm to keep your mind, stayed on Jesus.*

Lastly, we need SITUATIONAL SERENITY. No matter what comes, we need serenity. Serenity is peace of mind. The word peace means *Shalom* in Hebrew. In Hebrew, perfect means peace, peace. In the original translation, this is how this verse would read. "Thou wilt keep him in peace, peace, peace, whose mind is stayed on thee . . . ." I have to learn that whatever state I am in, to be content. This is what I want to leave with you, Isaiah is saying that if you trust in Him, and your mind, (*lifestyle*) is divine; His peace is your peace, now that is good news!

He wants us to realize that whatever we are going through, the same peace that His son had will be yours. I don't know about you, but that sounds mighty good. If I can just keep my mind stayed on Him, I will have that peace. The same peace that was displayed when people talked about Jesus. The same peace that was exhibited while he was being beaten by Roman soldiers. The same peace He had when his homeboy Judas betrayed Him. When I was younger in my parents' home on the wall hung a little plaque that said, *"God grant me the serenity to accept the things I cannot change, the courage to change the things I can, and the wisdom to know the difference"?* There is so much that crowds our mind that is actually a tool of the enemy. The more our minds are on worry, stress, issues, frustrations, the less it is on our God. Beloved, whenever we can place our minds on God; it creates a sense of serenity that can ease all of those who are unsettled.

4

I Know Who I Am

"And be not conformed to this world: but be

ye transformed by the renewing of your mind,

that ye may prove what is that good, and

acceptable, and perfect, will of God."

Romans 12:2

There is a multiplicity of people around the globe who have fallen victim to the malady of adaptation. Upon an individual being so engrossed in dressing, talking, teaching, singing, or even preaching like someone else; we can never be who God made us to be. When conformation takes place rather transformation, it leaves who we are and are to be vacated. When I think of the craft that God has blessed me with; I think of the great legacy of preachers such as: Dr. Cedric. D. Britt, Dr. C.A.W. Clark, Dr. C.B.T. Smith, and Dr. George Jackson, Jr. These giants rested in the gift God gave them and did not solely pattern themselves after others.

I would like to tackle two words in this second verse of the 12th chapter of Romans, in order for us to digest this discourse. I want for you to ponder the words transformed and conformed.

The word conformed suggests to us that what we are dealing with is simply a replica. While transformed affirms to us that it would be to create something, it becomes new from the inside out. Transformation deals with the inside. I will not let the outside dictate to me how I will act. I will not let it dictate to me how I feel, when to be happy, when to be sad, how I will dress. The Greek word for conformed is, *SIS-KAY-MY-TID-ZO*, with the root word being schema *(English—scheme).* This in turn means an underhanded plot. You change to match your surroundings, like a chameleon. Conformation deals with the outside. Conformation deals with men trying to be women and women trying to be men. It deals with children attempting to be grown up and grown-ups attempting to be children. A child can put on adult clothes, but their mind is still stuck in adolescent apperceptions *(or vice versa)*. A homosexual can wear women clothes, but his inner-mind will still be manlike. The schema conflicts with the inner man.

Here Paul gives us an anecdote for this assimilation. He raises the issue and then he gives us the resolution. He says, I do not want you to compromise your Christianity. I do not want you to give in to the takers. I do not want you to settle for the stingy. If you learn how not to conform but to transform, you will find God's will. There is a distinct difference between a pond and a river. Mosquitoes do not breed on moving bodies of rivers and mobile waters. They breed upon stalemated, stagnant and stilled waters. When we speak of stale, we are speaking of one not thinking for them self, but rather allowing someone else to think for them.

The mind here has been displayed as guilt that impedes our progress mentally. The reason we cannot achieve perfect status as the scripture prescribes, is because the deposit that was placed in us has been hidden due to guilt. That is why He says do not be like that, be like this, because of our past, but if I live it the way God wants me to live, then I will be who I know I should to be.

When God lives in you, you do not have to settle for the mediocrity of your surroundings. When God emanates through your mind, you check your environment and your environment no longer checks you. God has to free us from all of the demons that want us to be who they want us to be.

You have to have some *amness*. Every time they saw and heard from God he would say, I am the truth; I am the light; I am Alpha, Omega; I am the true vine. I am the first and I am the last. I am, I am, I am. The amness separates Him from everybody else. I don't have to be like you. Who are you? I don't want to look like you. Who are you? I don't want to think like you. Who are you? I know who I am! I don't have to drive your car. I know who I am. Stop trying to be like someone else, and be who you are. You should always have some amness in your life. Don't leave home without it! People spend time molding you to be so much like them, so that they can control your innermost thoughts, which happens to be your mind. This is what the world does. You take on the world's behaviors, mannerisms and thoughts. Then they occupy your mind.

In relationships, you come out of relationship and do not know who you are. It is because you became totally helpless. They controlled everything about you, your mind, thoughts, concepts and decisions. You have become so lost in what others expected from you, that you do not expect anything from yourself.

There have been times in all of our lives where we would do something, and then be lost to why we did it. You expressed something that did not originate from within. It does not represent what is on the inside, it came from an association. How can I have peace, when I have a jumper cable running from my mind to someone else's mind? If I give in to their mind, what do I do with my own mind? I disconnect my mind, and then focus on their mind. It is their life I am living, and not my own. What happens when they decide to dump you, whose mind do you go back to if you don't know who you are? They tell you, without me you are not going to be anything. But if your mind is connected to Him, He will *keep you in perfect peace, whose mind is stayed on Him.* Our problem is that we should look like what we shall be.

Two terms in the original language which deal with time and space. It really reads, Be not to time, but rather to eternity. Otherwise, we are to be more like the one who epitomizes eternity and not like those who are tied to time. There has to be a constant flow of thoughts, in order for me to be original in my own thoughts and not have to be like someone else. Renew your mind. If I do not think for myself, things begin to propagate in my mind that portray and are symbolic of things and people that are not like me. If you allow yourself to be like someone else, there is no one to be you. You do not create anything outside of your mind.

It is in your very mind where creativity is spawned and begun. If you do not believe me, why do you think God breathed into our mind? Because both nostrils lead to the brain. That is why he said, let this mind, because His thoughts are there, we just do not use it. Why couldn't He have breathed into our mouth? It is because there is no direct connectivity to the brain. The mouth points downward, but the nostrils points upward. In order to be who I am, God has to constantly renew me on the inside of my mind in order to keep me from adapting to who I am not. I have to be able to stand and be who I am no matter what is going on around me. I cannot live my life the way you want me to live it, because if I change for you, then who I am is left out in the cold. The Greek word for "perfect" is *telios,* which means that we are to have dominion, but because guilt messed up Adams response, the first Adam needed redemption. God created us to have dominion over everything. I cannot be controlled by my environment and have dominion over everything. *Where is your mind?* If anybody asks you who I am, I am not trying to be like Mike, I am trying to be like Christ!

Closing thought: "If that good is to be the proven conclusion and will; how can it emerge from the loins of sin?"

5

Are You Out Of Your Mind?

"Let this mind be in you,

which was also in Christ Jesus"

Philippians 2:5

In this chapter, I want to discuss the mind in a deeper sense. In a sense that would highlight the branches of the mind, which would really yield to us the product of what the mind should exude or display.

Mind in this text means attitude. Philippians 2:5, is about humility in the mind, essentially, one's attitude. I do not want you to miss this. You have always heard, your attitude determines your altitude. The attitude of Christ was to be about His father's business. He thought of others and not of Himself. If satan can give us a messed up attitude, he has won half the battle. What he fears the most, he attacks the most.

Think about it, satan gets most of us by getting us to develop an attitude concerning our gifts. Our gifts are only a deposit that others might withdraw from. We need to realize that we are only managers of that which has been deposited in us. When we have the attitude of, I have arrived, or should I say, nobody can preach like me, pull it like me, close like me, hoop like me, sing like me, pray like me, speak like me, we relieve humility and allow pride to reside. That is why the writer says in verse 4, look not on the things of yourself but rather on the things of others, because your fruit is not for you, it is for someone else!

Satan's attacks mark our assignment. Many times we are dismissed from our assignments, because our attitudes have sent word to our appointments, to cancel our arrival. When Jesus went back home to Nazareth, they attacked Him. The question that is being asked in this text is, why did Jesus go back? He went back because He wanted to help the people in the place He came from. He made special trips there to assist His acquaintances. His concern arises out of knowing where He came from; and then leading people out of what He left them in. It was not solely based upon where He was from geographically, it was psychologically, economically, and spiritually where He was from.

Our problem is that when God brings us from a place, we tend to forget the dilemma we were in, be it promiscuity, lying, backbiting, idolatry, wandering eyes and following acts. He went back to His hometown because this scripture says He took on the form of a servant and in the likeness of men. The word likeness, *hah-moy-a-mah*, means a copy. What keeps us from possessing this mind is that we desire suppressing what we should be expressing, and end up being repressing what is in our minds. Otherwise we tuck away our testimonies. We hide our helps, cover up our challenges, mismanage our maladies and misrepresent our mess-ups. If you have not been drug through hell, there is no way you can tell me what potholes to watch out for and how much dirt to expect, but when you are ready to share with me that you have been where I am going, you display the mind of Christ.

The great mind of Sigmund Freud speaks about the ego, superego, and the id. These concepts aid with the struggles that others are struggling with themselves. This scripture proves to me that God works on the theatre of my thoughts which is my attitude. God can hear our mind *(attitude)*. That is why He says, *"Let this mind . . ."*, because creators hear the imperfections and impediments in their creations. The mind is where decisions bully our destinations and ultimately our destiny. His mind seeks questions, whereas our mind seeks answers. What is the mind of Christ? W.W.J.D. *(What Would Jesus Do?)* This is essentially what Philippians 2:5 is saying to us. Let means *think*. If I think about food, then my mind envisions food because something must associate the mind with the matter. Jesus was humble. He is adorned in humility. There is so much responsibility entrusted to the word humility that it is one of the major components of a better world. II Chronicles 7:14, reminds us that you cannot pray for humility, but you need to be humble before you pray. I have a bee placed in my pulpit to remind me that I should be about what I preach about! There is a proverbial bee on the surface of this scripture. Otherwise, we should not just think about it, but be about it. Some may say that we are supposed to have the mind of Christ, NO, our finite, fickle and fallible frames could not contain the mind of Christ. But, we could possess the attitude of Christ.

Our attitudes are what others see and our mind is simply the projector. In other words, our attitudes are a direct reflection of what is going on in our mind. Think about someone that has a bad attitude. Nothing is considered or heard concerning their thoughts because their attitude is so nasty. When He says, *this,* it is as if there is a proverbial finger that arises from this text and points back to the text and says, THIS MIND. This particular pericopae was spoken demonstratively and in third person in a divine passive voice which is of God. Otherwise, God says Paul is not just speaking, he is repeating what I told him to say.

Closing thought: Don't let your that thwart your this . . . in other words, what you perfect is that, but what He perfects is THIS . . . in—means it becomes you and there is no more coaching it becomes culture! Our attitude is really a direct reflection of what we believe our needs are . . .

6

Do The Right Thing

"I find then a law, that, when I would do

good, evil is present with me."

Romans 7:21

This text is one of my favorites because it is a verse of transparency. This scripture really shows the struggle that is present in the lives of believers everywhere. I can remember so many different times in my own life where there was a proverbial tug of war going on mentally in my life.

To tussle and fight within one's mind does not mean that there is an imbalance psychologically; it simply suggests that the carnal is at war with spiritual. Whenever there is no struggle, the truth is that evil has probably already prevailed. Evil will never give up on overriding the spiritual, but if evil wins in your life, there will not be a fight to gain ground for the spiritual, you have to want it.

The word *that* rests between two commas and I would like to hurriedly share that in between two breaths lies death. The moment I decide to do good, sin is there to cause me to stumble. The deciding factor in whether or not we do the right thing or we do the wrong thing is predicated upon our minds. There is a war going on in our minds. It is not affecting my mind so much, but my thoughts are affected by evil cogitations. Otherwise, my mind is ok, but my thoughts are what I am trying to change. Thoughts are only participants on the battlefield of our mind.

Sometimes I wish that I could be placed under some anointed anesthesia and when I came to, everything will be alright. I would love to go into a sort of Christian-like coma and wake up and become the perfect Christian. But that is not the way God works. Consider the potter and clay in Jeremiah 18:3. God does not shape our minds, He shapes our thoughts. He made the vessel over again, because His thought showed a different picture. Our thoughts are the precursor to our minds. Sometimes the reason He continues to shape us, is because we are so ebuouyantly persistent to continue to do the same wrong thing *(Hebrews 13:5).* He has to mold us in order to get us to be what and who He wants us to be. When we are so tenacious and so adamant to do what we want to do, He has to intensify the process.

I have to be honest with you, I really need to level with you right here. I never knew that flesh was so difficult to control until I met God. Before I met God, I did not deal with these sorts of things. If I wanted to do it, I could do it and never turn back.

This is what I like to call the pulchritude and our libidinous drive. If I wanted to get it, I got it and was proud that I had it. If I desired it, there was no devil in hell that was going to stop me from getting it. But now that God has shown up, we find that when we do not resist wrong, He has to mold us a little harder and that is when we feel the pain. I have come to find out that I want what I want, when I want it.

Consequently and evidently what God does when I am hell-bent on getting it is, He allows me, but He protects me in allowing me. There are others I am are sure that He has allowed doing many things in your life that you know you had no business doing, but He protected you all the while. You had sexual encounters, but you did not get a disease. You experimented with drugs, but you did not overdose. You drove drunk, but you did not have a wreck. You skipped school, but you still passed the class. You had a gambling habit, but you still paid the bills. He protected you even when he allowed you. I found out that if He had not allowed me to go through it, I would still be trying to get it right now. What I wanted God to do was disconnect the cables of this flesh I really do not want to fool with it. Flesh has me doing some things I am not so proud of. Your flesh will have you in some places that you normally would not go. I have discovered that sometimes you have to almost lose your mind in order for Him to change your mind. The Lord is not going to move some thing's in our life in order for us to walk the way we should walk, he will sit you right in the midst of the mess and watch you maneuver through it.

We see that even in the secular society. If I was to call a secular witness, he would say, "my mind is telling me no but my body is telling me yes." The body, mind, heart and soul are different but they are all one in the same. If the enemy can get us to commit suicide in our cogitations or our thoughts, he has assassinated the very opportunity for us to win the war. My mind was made up to do right, but wrong caused a gravitational pull. I became a robber in my religious rationale. I found myself expressing my explanation through eradicated and explicit expletives; otherwise I give them a piece of my mind!

The word *then* in Greek means, *Ar-ah*, to draw a conclusion after the conclusion. My mind was made up previously. There are three different levels of consciousness that we must acknowledge. The conscious mind is like the tip of an iceberg, where only a small part of the iceberg is seen protruding out of the water. The preconscious mind is like the water around the iceberg, it is the part that we most time ignore. The unconscious mind is like the massive part of the iceberg that lies beneath the water that we cannot see. Great dangers lurk in what is not seen. In this translation, there is a logical resemblance and coordinating conjunction of deduction and subsiding. Otherwise, you will never fully see what is in the mind, until what you can see has subsided, or you miss the obvious while looking at the tip of the iceberg.

Closing thought: I want to tell you our problem . . .

our problem is our then needs to be our now; but

because our now is then;

it almost ends up being too late!

7

There's No Place Like Home

"And when he came to himself, he said, How

many hired servants of my father's

have bread enough and to spare,

and I perish with hunger!"

Luke 15: 17

Leaving home is sometimes a hurried act, full of

anticipation and weighed down with curiosity and

that brings a myriad of lessons. For most, home

is better coming to, than it is leaving from. The young man in this text has done what so many of us have done, he left home. Inasmuch as he left home, the initial lesson that I believe he would to share with us, is that he never should have left home in the first place. The issues at home, the problems in our marriage, the struggles on our jobs, and the circumstances in our churches would be so much better if we would learn to evaluate where we are before we leave, rather than have to reflect on where we were. I would like to approach this very familiar passage from a different perspective.

This young man's issue was not the mere fact that he left home. His issue was not that he asked of his father to divide the goods. His issue was not that he spent all living riotously. Believe it or not, his issue was not about the fact that he was about to eat the husks that the swine did eat. His issue was not that he thought about it and came to himself. It was not even moment that he finally returned home. His issue was that he was not at himself. He was literally and mentally out of his mind. It has been deemed years ago that a mind is a terrible thing to waste. When one loses their mind, they ultimately lose their life.

This parable is a perfect example of how messed up your life can become when you are out of your mind. I need not alarm anyone in the reading of this book, but I need to hurry and let you know that whenever you began to think selfishly, you become prodigal.

The word prodigal simply means wasteful. Any person that wastes anything will ultimately be in want. Waste always precedes want. Think about a person who wastes their youthfulness, they want it back. A person who wastes money, they want it back. Anyone that has had a good man or woman, they want them back. Someone that has had the ideal job and lost it, they want it back. Many of us abandon our places of responsibility, because we are out of our minds. Sin causes a type of madness that warps our minds. Watch the word play here in the text. He gathered **ALL** together, he went to a FAR country, **RIOTOUS** living, spent **ALL**, mighty famine in **THAT** land, **HE** began to be in want. Verse 16 says, "no man gave unto **HIM**". It was *there* that the famine happened, they had necessary things, but he did not.

First, there can be no true appreciation without any real complications. Now understand this, his mind was on himself rather than on his father. This is where the mind slip took place. Whenever your mind is taken off of Him it is on the wrong thing.

This young man was only to receive these things when his father had died. But he wants something he has not yet earned. Some people want the prize without the pain. How could he mentally and psychologically ask his father for something that should come when his father has not yet died? But, he asks for it while his father yet lives. How is it that you desire to have what I have, and yet you have not dealt with the hurt and pain it took me to get it? Some people want the hallelujah, without the heartache. They want the thank you Jesus, without the Lord have mercies. They want to give the praise report, without first submitting the prayer requests. You cannot handle the goods without the groans. You cannot handle the anointing without the affliction. That is why the writer says in Psalms 119, *"It was good for me that I was afflicted, that I may learn my statutes."*

You have to go through some things in order to appreciate what He has for you. Secondly, realization plus cultivation equals activation. Activation means to make sense. You cannot arrive at a place without first having left a place. This young man came to himself and said, I am crazy to be down here eating like pigs and my daddy has better for me at home. He is still talking to himself, but now he is talking sense to himself. He ultimately says, I am going to get up from here and go home and say to my daddy, I spoke to you wrong. I spoke to your representative wrong. I was talking out of the side of my mouth, I cannot be identified as your offspring and acting the way I was acting. He was about to partake in something that should not be in him and I can almost hear him saying, behind yonder blue hills, away in the dim distance, lies my father's house, a house of many mansions, and full supplies that the servants have bread enough and even some to spare.

Sometimes we play a part in things we have no business being a part of, because that is not how

God created us to be. Whenever you do not have the right thought patterns you will ultimately eat with the hogs. That is why He said, *"let this mind be in you"*. When you think with your mind outside of His mind, you will eat below your gift every time. Lastly, your intonation will ultimately impede His declaration.

When this young man said, *give me*, he spoke to his father in a tone in which he should not have. We cannot and will not receive the true things God has for us until we are at ourselves. Yes, he received what he asked for when he left home, but it was nothing in comparison to what he received when he returned home. He left a palace, went to a pit and returned to a party. There is no place like home.

To contact the Author:

Pastor M.E. Lyons

Email: revmelyonsone@aol.com

Pastor M.E. Lyons: (214) 641-8115

Pastor's Office: (936) 634-6060

Mailing Address:

P.O. Box 0690

Lufkin, Texas 75901

Goodwill Missionary Baptist Church

812 East Lufkin Avenue

Lufkin, Texas 75901

Other Book(s) Written/Published

Fresh Air Volume One

"The mind; the pulpit of God" is an intriguing and thought provoking subject. The author suggests that God uses man's mind as His pulpit. One truly must use his or her mind to grasp what the author portrays in the preface of this book. I am eagerly awaiting the completion of this book to see how the author enlarges on the premises found in this preface."

Doctor S.L. Curry, Jr.

New Zion Missionary Baptist Church ~

Winona, TX

"It is a fact! What we spend most of our time thinking about is what we become! If we spend most of our time thinking about secular things, then that is where our priorities lie! Or we can choose to think about Spiritual things. It is up to us! What we choose determines our destiny! This book is a wonderful guide in helping us to make the right decision!"

Mayor Jack Gorden

City of Lufkin, TX

"The principles established in this book will help challenge the minds of those who have a desire to exercise God's truth that ministry might become purposeful and fruitful as the mind is cultivated by God. This book will inspire you to listen for the voice of God as you have been assigned to become the tangible hands and feet of His Son, Jesus Christ."

Pastor Rodney McFarland, Jr.

Hebron Missionary Baptist Church ~

Longview, TX

"An outstanding leader sent by God will always want to share the compelling Good News with God's people. This humble servant Leader will encourage us through his writing. God has allowed our paths to cross and I am happy about that. May God bless you Pastor M.E. Lyons in all of your endeavors."

Bishop Leroy Shankle, Sr. DD.

Presiding Prelate of The Church
by Christ Jesus, Inc.

"Dr. Lyons has ventured into an area where many preachers have dared to matriculate. It is evident that he has pressed his ear to the mouth of God and the expectation is that many will find release as a result of allowing God to mount the pulpit of their mind."

Bishop Kenneth White

Linconia Tabernacle Christian Center

United Holy Church of America

Trevose, PA

Pastor M.E. Lyons lives in the piney woods of East Texas in the city of Henderson, Texas. He is married to the former LaTish Luckey, and they have three beautiful children: Déjà, Myron and Jeremiah. He loves to read, write and study the Word of God. He has attended Dallas Institute of Funeral

Services, D. Edwin Johnson Baptist Seminary, and Oxford University in London, England with Post Graduate Studies in Homiletics, Hermeneutics, with emphasis on examination of scripture. He is currently seeking a Masters Degree in Psychology at Kaplan University. He has authored one book, Fresh Air Volume One.